SURRENDERING

INTO

LOVE

SURRENDERING

INTO

LOVE

Heart Opening Verses

of Ecstasy & Wonder

KRISTEN D'AMATO

Come to Life
Los Angeles, CA

© 2024 Kristen D'Amato

Cover and book design by Kristen D'Amato
Printed in the United States of America

Names: D'Amato, Kristen, author.
Title: Surrendering into Love: Heart Opening Verses
of Ecstasy & Wonder
ISBN 979-8-9903041-0-9

www.kristendamato.com

Ebook ISBN 979-8-9903041-1-6
Audiobook ISBN 979-8-9903041-2-3

Go raibh míle maith agat

CONTENTS

AUTHOR'S NOTE

Recently, I had a profound experience of surrender that left me with my heart blown open and in an altered state for several days and nights where these verses streamed through me at all hours of the day. I could hear them in my dreams and woke in the middle of the night to write them down. Only to be awoken again at daybreak with another stream of several verses.

During this time, the only thing that mattered was allowing the voice of divine grace to flow through and dance along the page. It was a way to encapsulate a slice of what I was experiencing and translate it into a form that could become a tool of invitation and remembering of the beauty that is here for us all to partake in.

We are divine beings, my friends, and this can be so easily forgotten by the minutiae of life's tasks. Yet there is a portal always available that can instantaneously transport us into a world of wonder. This is the way of the heart. May these verses soak into your soul and bathe it in the light of love and the sweetness of the ecstasy of surrender.

These poems are the result of receiving touch imbued with a whole lot of consciousness. It doesn't require other substances to take you to heights beyond that which you have known. Look deeply into the eyes of another and see yourself and the divine reflected back. When you allow yourself to let go, and let go some more, you enter a world where everything is possible.

Kristen D'Amato
March 2024
Los Angeles, CA

HOW TO USE THIS BOOK

These poems are a transmission of love.
I channeled them in the days following
an experience of profound surrender and
union with the essence of Oneness with
the Divine and my body. Another soul
assisted me in activating states of ecstasy.
However, this is not required to achieve
profound and ecstatic states of surrender.

These verses are in the exact form that
they came through. I did not change
anything, including the order. There is
some repetition in the language,
however, I did not want to diversify it

because I wanted to preserve the purity
of the transmission. This collection, from
the first poem to the production of the
paperback and audiobook, took place
over one lunar cycle commencing just
after the new moon in February of
2024.

A way to enjoy this book is to use each
poem as a contemplation. Read it and
allow whatever questions, thoughts and
sensations that arise to bubble up. Notice
what the words stir in you.

As I was in the final stages of layout, a
message came through from the angels to
accompany the poetry. It was comprised
of 6 simple steps for living an ecstatic life.

6 STEPS TO LIVING AN ECSTATIC LIFE

Immerse yourself in wonder.

Take each day as a gift no matter what comes or what is happening around you. Have the strength and courage to reframe it this way. It works wonders.

Ask questions that guide you to the essence of joy.

What is most meaningful to you and why?
How do you like to be touched?
When is a time you remember being loved?

What makes you cry tears of joy?
When was the last time you experienced
divine awakening?
These types of questions return you to
(and keep you rooted in) the heart.

You are a divine being of light.
Don't ever forget this. Walk through
your days knowing this is a fact.
All else dissolves when this is
remembered.

Ask questions surrounding what
sparks inspiration.
Lean into the dark places first and gather
data for transmuting these messages into
light. They are codes of love, divine

messengers AKA inspiration. It is easier than you think. Plumb the depths regularly and be present with what is there.

Ask your heart what it is most afraid of.

Listen. Allow the emotional energy to move and be refreshed by presence. This leads to joy and expression.

You are here to make peace with whatever was.

Let the past go – graciously, with gratitude and kindness for all.

Here's how to do it:
Ask yourself where hurt still lingers in

your heart. Work with the first hurt that arises.

Stay present as you gently, lovingly and kindly explore why you are still hurt. There is a day when this hurt is no longer there. That day, that moment is now.

Imagine a glowing ball of light, entering your heart, and filling it with the greatest love you have ever known, or could imagine. Let this light permeate every cell of your being. Watch as it works its way through you, one area at a time, following a pace that allows total saturation. All that remains is the purest essence of you - the truth of who you are.

Revel in this.

Feel the change.

You are here to accept love into your
heart.
There are many things and many people
who may have told you otherwise.
It is time now to set these lies aside and
KNOW your goodness.

Lie down and allow this light of love to
penetrate every ounce of your being.
Feel the sensations, allow guidance to
come through to help with places that
feel stuck or congested. Call on them for
help. Do this now.
Wait and allow.

Breathe deep breaths from your belly all
the way up your chest. Inhale through

your nose, expanding your belly, rib cage and shoulders. Exhale slowly through the mouth. Take deep breaths, allowing the light to work through you.

Keep going until you feel complete – peaceful – calm – revitalized – awake.

This is how to begin allowing trust back into your life in a fuller way.

It is important to establish trust within yourself, for yourself, by yourself (and with the support of your angelic guardians.) This practice will help you feel alive and connected to the truth of who you are – your divine essence.

Tell the world your story.

We are here to delight in the company of others. Somewhere there is someone who can benefit from hearing your perspective, your experience of life. When you choose to share, it is an act of generosity. It is a gift you give. It is a kindness and offering that adds a frequency of love to the grid of collective consciousness.

Tell all the stories even the painful ones, especially the painful ones. The greatest healing can come from knowing we are not alone, that we belong to this magnificent web of life.

Take this wisdom, these six steps, and apply them to your everyday life to spark inspiration and to remember your divine essence as you revel and wonder at this incredulous gift we get to experience called life.

THE VERSES

GRAND RISING

I died in your arms last night.

Last night I was born anew.

There is before you and after you.

A grand reset,

A grand rising.

From flesh what was before

no longer applies

everything has changed

since looking in your eyes.

I have longed for this my whole life

I have known it to be true

felt a calling in my cells,

driving me to remember

my body

as a vehicle

for divine embrace.

I knew it was possible

and yet I doubted it too.

Years of waiting, wanting, fearing

opening my heart

to have it dismantled

by wrongdoing.

Trust is restored

more than ever before.

We healed lifetimes, lineage lines.

This gift we made

transcends us.

We are making a mark,

taking a stand

for love

and royal sexuality

as a way to transcend the mind

feel the body divine.

Every moment of every day

is filled with rapture.

Slow down,

pause

and listen.

BECOMING

You've just never been loved by a man

who knows how to love you.

I now know this to be true.

In just one night, a moment in time,

all the pain and confusion fell away

clarity came

that I can love a man

worship a man,

desire a man,

fully welcome a man.

For my whole life
I've been asking the wrong question.
It never was,
can I truly love a man?
It is who is a man that knows how
to love all of me?

This pivot is sending monumental quaking
through the framework of my being.
My life was built upon this question
and in a flash
it's incinerated
by the presence of you.

I'm in the midst of realigning
to this new frequency.

Part of me still can't believe it's possible,
can't believe it's true.

My tears gently wash away the residue
of what was
revealing what I am
what I am
becoming.

FREEDOM

I always thought it was me

yet I open to you

so freely

with the freedom

that transcends time, expands space

and touches the truth.

Our soul's dancing among the candlelit

flames throwing shadows on the wall

I see you

I see it all.

The darkness that comes over you

in your eyes

when I invite you to ravish me

you take me fully with your eyes.

freedom

freedom

FREEDOM.

HOMECOMING

Calling all parts of me

calling me home.

You're safe now

you're welcome

you are wanted here

in this body.

I never loved you.

I love you now.

I know how.

I give you this home

this sacred temple

divinely crafted

to house all of you.

Sweet girl

I saw you, we heard you

now you get to play.

Go on the vacation of your dreams.

You earned it.

You've been holding fear for so long.

I know now how to take great care of you.

Precious one.

This fully embodied woman is now

the Queen of this temple.

You can lay down your armor

and return to innocence.

LUMINOSITY

Oh, radiant one

I feel you

pour through me

lighting my lantern

with your oil of love.

Ecstasy pours through

like the light touches the day

and the stars grace the sky each night.

This is what it is to be alive.

Half life, no more

luminosity reigns

down

upon me

now.

PLATTER OF DELIGHT

Eat up on me.

This platter of delight

delivers a feast

only purity of presence can taste.

Will you join me now

to traverse universes

in an ecstatic explosion

of remarkable sweetness

where time slows

the beating wings of a hummingbird

to stillness

enraptured in full sensual awareness

by the smell

of nectar

floating on the wind.

THE ALCHEMY OF US

The alchemy of us

is liquid gold

upon a mantle of desire

that transcends all powerlessness

into absolute bliss

at being alive.

To hear, know, and be

the cosmic heartbeat

pulsing with freedom

elation

transmutation

of shadows that kept us small.

We are gods and goddesses

sisters and brothers

to this all.

In this state of emanation

we create

a space

where freedom resides

as the fuel for change.

The spark of hope

kindled into a raging bonfire

upon which

the cauldron of our love

takes the shape

of a phoenix in the night

flying high above

our outstretched arms

in reverent belonging

singing praises

'Free at last,

free at last

thank God almighty

we are free at last.'

THE TEMPLE OF OUR LOVE

The temple of our love

has walls made of glass

all is visible

can you feel me now?

Do you sense the way

your love translates

into my body,

into my being?

You create a tidal wave

of longing, hope, desire

all inside a prayer

to be transmitted

beyond the borders of our flesh.

The temple of our love

is a field where everything

that once was is laid to rest.

We are committed to a new way

of being seen

that is as ancient as the roots

of the great Sequoia trees.

Standing tall and proud in time

you found me waiting

bowing at the feet

of a river of light

lifting me in a warm embrace

saying,

all is welcome here

all is welcome love,

you need not be afraid

in the temple of our love.

AN ODE TO DESIRE

Desire fuels my everything.

Without it, life is dry

like a desert

little life resides.

The flora and fauna of my heart

are a rainforest

overflowing,

teeming with water and life

nurtured by my choices.

Drawing upon the well

is a constant blossoming

enriched by presence, appreciation and

love.

Feel me now.

Hear me now.

I call out to you

to return

ever present

to your home

of thriving.

RADIANCE OF THE HEART

There was before you

and after you.

In this space in between

I transformed

unrecognizable

to what I once was

now vibrating

in the stellar radiance

of the heart.

TEACH ME

Teach me.

Oh wise one,

teach me your soul

your way

of being

of this world.

And for this,

I will honor you.

I will bless you

with my love.

TRANSCENDENCE

You are here now

with me.

Together we transcend

all space and time

into Oneness

fullness

allness.

This is everything.

TAKE ME HOME TONIGHT

Will you take me

home tonight

to that place

where love lights a path

that circles

lovers dancing

naked

under the wildness

of the moon?

Will you take me

home tonight

to the place

where lovers play

imitating sounds of the wild?

Will you take me

home tonight

to the place

where beauty is in everything

and we are

exactly where we are meant to be?

Will you take me

home tonight

lover

in your arms

I delight

at the magic

of the universe?

I bow my head before you

glorious one

in my home tonight.

LANGUAGE OF LIGHT

The language of light

moves through me.

It finds a way

to express

divine intelligence

intertwines with

places of reverence

like our hearts beating

in time

with the sacred union of life.

This language of light

will take you

on a ride

to where your heart

has longed to go.

It knows the way

it carries you slowly

one word to the next

a string of pearls

illuminated with

the sacredness of all life.

This language of light

brings a message:

You, divine soul,

are worthy of expressing

your exquisite nature.

There is nothing

in this world

that can stop you

from experiencing

the pleasure and ecstasy

of divine union

with source energy.

We are one.

We always were.

We always will be.

ARMS OF GRACE

Regal oneness is alive in me now.

Fear is conquered

in the loving arms of divine grace.

Will you lie with me

quietly in exquisite bliss?

As the winds blow

and the earth quakes

we know no bounds.

It is quiet now

in this house of love.

ONCE AGAIN

Lasting breaths of you linger

in the air of my home.

I breathe you in

and thank you once again.

We transcended thoughts

deeply engrained

that had us feeling

anything but whole.

Hold me now

once again

in your divine embrace.

Whisper to me

this question of surrender.

Remind me of this place

where you and I meet

in infinite possibility.

BREATHE

Breathe, breathe you say.

Breathe in the delight

of this day.

Each pleasurable moment

sounds like a singing bowl

resounding through each cell.

Breathe, breathe in the day.

Each sacred scent

tantalizing textures

that create

36

scripts of whole new worlds.

Breathe, breathe in the way

you mark me

with irrevocable sweetness.

Feel it deeply,

fully,

completely.

Breathe in this precious moment.

You are here now

to experience all the sensations

of this glorious human life.

BOWING AT THE FEET OF LOVE

This is a moment

when an outpouring of love

changes everything.

Galaxies are created

kindness is found.

Life, oh life

show me how

to bow down

to every moment

of every day

at the blessed feet

of love.

Savor each moment.

Once you are found,

you will not be lost again.

DO YOU KNOW ME NOW?

I walk into the light

the divine essence of our play.

Skin touches skin

shimmering delight

reflected upon the window sill.

There is a bird

who sings songs of simplicity and grace.

Do you know me now

that we have found each other

in the stillness

of the night?

THE ANGELS CAME TO PLAY

The angels came to play.

They lay a kiss upon your lips

and let you know there is nothing

to fear in love.

The angels came to play.

They held my feet

bearing witness

to expansion of my vessel

more space to create.

The angels came to play.

They enveloped me in blessings.

Oh, this day the angels came to play

I was forever changed.

TOUCHED BY A MAN

I had no idea

it could be so easy

to be touched by a man.

I long had doubts

I could ever trust a man

with my heart.

So much time I proved

this story right.

How wrong I was.

Now I know

how beautiful it is

to be touched by a man.

BEACONS

Decades

generations

healed in one night

in one leap of faith

from one courageous soul

to another

this is the way

to transform shame

in this world.

We stand enveloped in love.

We are not alone

many stand

alongside us

in a celebratory line

watching our every move

initiating our paths

forward into

explosions of light

of life.

It is our time

to shine our light

as beacons

guiding

lost souls home.

SOUL FOOD

Your love

is food for my soul

nourishing me

beyond previous recognition.

The light of love

transcends time and space

with its exquisite nature,

I ride the rays

Into

a future of brighter days

than I thought possible.

Sing with me now

divine lover

as we bow before the altar

of our souls.

GLASS HOUSE

In this glass house

of my heart

I welcome all

who walk

the path home

to where courage is

the fuel beneath

the cauldron of desire

as we dance

naked and wild underneath

the moonlit sky.

A RECIPE FOR THE HEART

A recipe for the heart

begins with

a dose of

ecstatic encouragement

that plumbs

the depths of

regions denied

only to shine

a light

on magnificent

crystals that have

taken shape within.

We are here

to take the time

to cherish these

precious gemstones,

the jewels

of our desires.

ARRIVAL

Divine union

lights the way

for more preciousness

than ever before.

My heart is caressed

into ecstatic pleasure

emanating with joy.

This pulse is alive in me now.

I sense the breath of life

surrounding all that exists.

THE PLACE WE GO

There is a place we go

where universes are made

among spiraling

flecks of dust

you can see

a sparkle of light

throbbing with delight.

The place where everything

is made

comes to life

here.

IN YOUR ARMS

My heart cries out

a joyful cry

this is the place we go to die

a thousand little deaths

in your arms tonight.

Your body moves

against mine

in slow synchronous time

divine orchestration

conducted by God.

You whisper to my heart

an invitation

to let it all go.

Pulsing with the breath of life

I died in your arms tonight.

PALACE OF WONDER

Between my legs

lies a palace of wonder.

You need not fear

this place where all creation exists.

Let desire

burn away

thoughts of capturing

that which can never be caged.

Wildness reigns free

among the creatures of the night

enticing courage, trust and destiny

to be the belt

of this constellation

in a sky

of timeless expression.

Beyond you or I

we go to find

peace of mind,

stillness of heart

where our souls can craft

a cosmic dance.

Will you meet me there,

Beloved one,

in this palace of wonder?

LAY YOUR SORROWS TO REST

Mother earth

rains down the sorrows

of the world.

She carves a way

to the ocean

where they play

in the primordial waves

where all is welcome.

There is no darkness to dark for the sea.

She whispers words of

sweetness and understanding

that dissolve

tears into Oneness.

Come here when you want to cry,

lay your sorrows to rest

in the loving embrace of the Mother.

OH GLORIOUS ONE

Oh glorious one

you've touched my soul

in a myriad of ways.

Won't you walk with me

now among this cavern

of delight

where jewels of ecstasy

light the way

to places beyond

what our minds could imagine

where only purity

of the heart

reigns.

LIGHT SONG

I will meet you among the trees

anytime.

You name the date

and I will be there

to walk with

the ancient ones

and bask in their glory

as they whisper

light songs in our ears

that only the stars have heard before.

For we have gathered

enough light between us

to decipher this

precious code of life

carrying lifetimes

of stories

of those who came before us.

We ride upon

this newfound glory

of life that exists beyond

where the light songs

are all that remain.

BECKONING

Hear me, hear me now.

I beckon for you

in the darkness

to shine your light this way

so I can see truth

beyond measure

where everything

comes into focus.

My chest rising and falling

now with the calm breaths

of absolute knowing.

Where shall we go next,

Beloved One

to light up the waves

with our bioluminescent steps

as we dance a prayer of devotion

to all that's come before

and all that's yet to pass?

In love

I surrender

and bow down at the feet

of what remains.

You, master of life,

show me now

take me to the place

where only hearts know

where the stars

of these stars

kiss the nape of the radiant ones

who guide us home

again and again.

DELICIOUSNESS OF LIFE

I don't know where this leads

I just take the next expansive step

following my heart song

as I walk

in wonder and awe

among

the deliciousness of life.

PEARLS

There is no place

I'd rather be

than here with you, now.

Will you let me follow

and you lead the way

to where tiny grains of sand

become pearls

upon the neck

of the divine goddess?

EMERGENCE

I have emerged

better than I could have possibly imagined

with such ease and tranquility.

I know now

that what I want is within my reach.

I've waited decades

maybe lifetimes

to taste the sweetness

of surrender

in the way

that I remembered

from an era long ago.

MOONLIGHT

My soul wants to dance

with yours

under the moonlight

in the water.

Take me with you

into waves of ecstasy

and pleasure

beyond

where we have

ever gone

before.

WATERFALL OF LIGHT

Like a waterfall of light

you pour through me

waking me in the night

again and again

in ecstatic expression

of divine remembrance.

BEAUTY

I awaken on this day

buzzing with gratitude

for the raw truth

that beauty

is an alive and pulsing force

that drives miracles

beyond recognition.

Will you open your heart

to let beauty have its way?

CHEST OF LIGHT

The next invitation

to surrender

is here.

You need not be afraid.

You are safe now.

You know the beauty

that waits for you

on the other side

as you walk

through these halls

of darkness

into the unknown.

Remember me,

I'm holding your hand

in the gloriousness

of each moment.

Your presence

is all

that is needed

to transmute

all fear

into the impulse

77

that creates universes.

Come child,

walk with me now

through this shadow

of darkness.

Together

we will meet

and delight in all

the discomfort

knowing the treasures

that lie within

this chest of light.

LABOR

This next wave of

surrender is beckoning

me now.

You need not contract

remember how it is done.

Open

Soften

Breathe

Allow.

You have got this.

An awakening is upon you.

Expression of your truest essence

is the only option now.

Allow, allow, allow

freedom to take the place of fear.

It is here.

There is nothing more to do

except breathe

and allow.

BEARING WITNESS

Being witnessed by you

has been one of the greatest

gifts I've ever known.

Your attention,

your absolute presence

unlocked an unfolding

more beautiful

than I could ever have imagined.

This is me

you see

now

naked

I bare my soul.

VEIL OF YOUR SURRENDER

There is something

more magnificent

than you can imagine

waiting for you

through the veil

of your

surrender.

WONDER

Rise, rise

beautiful one

into this glorious day

where the sun kisses

the wings of the butterfly

and bees dance

their way to

the nectar of life.

Will you meet

each moment of this day

with curiosity

allowing your inner child

to delight

in playful wonder?

THE NEXT EXPRESSION

In my heart of my will

lies an ember

waiting to be fanned

into the flame

it once was.

A child of innocence

that knows

nothing past or to come

just pure presence

and desire

to uncover

the next expression

of the heart's delight.

THE NAKEDNESS OF TRUTH

We circle each other

in this circle dance of life

quietly, slowly

removing one garment at a time.

The weight of lifetimes

gently releasing

received by the surety

of the Mother's

steadfast embrace.

Where are you now

in the nakedness of truth?

Surrounded

by the loving light

of angel songs

singing us back

to the place

we call home.

Where all that resides

is beauty

eloquently expressed

in a lyrical melody

that brings tears

to our eyes

every time

we welcome it in.

BIRTHING

In this labor
I move through lifetimes.
My ancestors rally on the sidelines
cheering me on with gracious smiles.

Through each contraction
and release of my will
I surf waves
of birthing a whole new me.

Free from all that came before
distilled down to an essence
of pure presence and love.

RODEO OF LIFE

Will you take a chance

and ride in this rodeo of life

where spirits are not broken or tamed?

Rather, wildness and freedom

become the way

to move in tandem

among both beauty

and the beast.

NEW LIFE

Take me home

to the place of innocence and play

where we meander

among tantalizing tendrils of life

bursting forth

in ecstatic assurance

that the Sun

will welcome them

each day

with an opportunity

for growth

renewal

nourishment

and light.

Oh, this precious life.

It feels so good to be alive

and get to revel

in the divine orchestration

beyond anything

the mind could ever conjure.

This magic is alive

in us now

always

waiting to be recognized.

Will you

take the chance

to welcome new life

in each moment

exhaling

all that no longer serves

the pure intentions

of your soul?

SHADOW DWELLERS

There are places

where our shadows dwell.

They feast upon

unspoken fears

waiting to be witnessed.

Until then,

they moan, they cry, they wreak havoc

scrambling through the

chambers of our hearts

banging on the walls

for recognition.

Will you welcome them

into the temple of your heart

and feed them tenderness instead?

ANGER

Hear me now

says a voice inside.

You have gone lifetimes

shushing me, putting me aside.

What you don't know

is I am the fuel for all your desires.

Welcome me into your open arms

where I can lay my head

upon your balmy chest.

Together we will soar

as one soul united

inside a framework of compassion.

Tell me,

what do you desire most?

Set me free

and you will find

I dance a wild dance

spitting flames

throwing fire.

And you, my dear,

are the source from whence it came.

You are the sorceress

committed to change

hammering me into precision blades.

An architecture designed to house all of me

refined into fires of transmutation

transfiguration

an exquisite alchemy

of elemental preciousness

valued beyond measure.

You will find

that when you welcome me

into the house of your heart

we can move worlds.

A MOMENT'S TIME

In a moment's time

everything can change.

All you once imagined

can be true in an instant.

Are you ready

to take a leap of faith

into the chasm

of your heart's truest desires?

55

Oh my tender heart

walk with me

as I hold your hand gently

and tell you how much I love you.

You are a miracle

born of light

each day expanding and contracting

into a stellar display

that takes the breath away

from anyone blessed to witness

your wild purity of expression.

An exaltation

singing praises,

a declaration

wailing aloud,

an excitation

leaping joyously

into unknown terrain,

where inspiration is born

and flows free

like a raging river at sunset.

CHASM OF THE HEART

I am enthralled

with the way

words dance upon your tongue

and the touch of your fingertips

lights up worlds

beneath my skin.

Will you come to me now

and lay your head

up on my chest

so each rising breath

can be a song

singing you a lullaby

of truth?

If you choose

to venture deeper

into this realm of the unknown

with me

I know we will find

places unimaginable

that awaken

dormant codes of light

a celestial activation

waiting to happen.

The choice is yours.

Are you willing to take a leap

deeper into the chasm of the heart

than you have ever gone before?

EYE OF THE STORM

I reside now

in this place of calm

the eye of the storm

where chaos swirls around me

and I remain

steady in my presence

in my love

and when debris comes in

I welcome it

and allow my breath

to carry it home

into the dissolution

of Oneness.

SYMPHONY OF PLEASURE

Imagine your insides

gilded with gold

soft and supple

liquid golden light

your heart and lungs

pulsing with the elixir of life.

Each breath in

each heartbeat

is a testament to the miracle

that resides within you.

Will you seize this day

by remembering

your ecstatic nature?

Will you open

to the possibility

of the perfection of life?

There is a divine template

alive, within you now

unfolding in perfect accord.

Can you hear it

humming,

harmonizing

with the birds,

flowers and trees

beckoning you to listen

to the grand symphony

of pleasure?

HEIGHTS

Oh, sweet man

will you take me to the heights

where birds are soaring

and the flap of their wings

against the air

is an ecstatic dance

between the molecules

of the spaciousness of the sky

and the delicate plumage

of each barb of feather?

Will you take me to that place

where time stops

and everything in existence

resides

between our eyes?

STARS OF THE STAGE

Step aside mind.

It's time

for body and heart

to be the stars of the stage

delivering an epic performance

of dalliance

that untethers

the source

of truest expression.

This is a dance

of exquisite articulation

a song crafted

from the purest intentions.

Watch in awe

at the Grace

that pours through me now.

Be a witness

and participant

in this delicacy

of co-creative mastery.

The lights have dimmed.

Are you ready

to go on?

THE GIFT

Every moment

of every day

is a miracle.

Recognize the vessel

of your heart

golden and glimmering

with life.

Each inhalation

and each exhalation

is a reminder of this miracle.

Meet the day where you are

allow your senses

to keep you connected

with the truth of who you are.

Raise a glass in celebration

to the glorious gift

given

to you.

SPRING

You found your way

to me

through intoxicating scents

of hyacinths and wild roses.

Two hawks circle one another

in a courting dance

before climbing

upon the back of the other

to be carried away

by the winds of creation.

Steadfast and stunning,

this is the coming

of spring.

ERA OF SURRENDER

Rebirth
regeneration
shedding of skins
to be composted
dissolved
back into
nourishment
for the soul.

I climb
higher and higher
I'm not looking back now.

I've reached the final mile
of this long time marathon.

Across the finish line,
I laugh and cry.
I made it.

I made it here
to this place I dreamed of
and it is far better
than I could have possibly imagined.

Dissolution, Oneness, Divine Union
call it what you will.
Now I know.
Now I remember.

There is no turning back now.

I have arrived
in a new era
of surrender.

WOMB WHISPERS

Cradled in my bosom

my womb whispers

messages

of love, kindness and care.

Do you hear them?

Do you receive them?

They're calling you home

to grace.

MESSAGES OF LOVE

Come with me
into this timeless space
where magic reigns
and freedom holds our hands
as we walk along
the edges of places
known and unknown.

Here
and only here,
you will become awakened
by the words
of God's embrace.

Do you hear messages

coming through for you now?

They speak of love
and show you how
to know yourself
better than you've known yourself
before.

WE KNOW THIS PLACE

We are engaged

in a fine play of the heart

where we roam

among the flowers

as they transmit

their codes of delicate delight

pulsing with light.

Something in the current

we ride

to the place

our ancestors called home.

SECRETS OF LIFE

Full moon rises
sun sets
here among the shadows
stories unfold
of remembering.

Where are you now?

Do you dance
in the luminous light
that shines silvery
on the curves of the earth?

Are you dancing

in dreams

as I whisper words of love

that awaken you

to the awe

that finds a home

nestled in your ears?

A smile of recognition

graces your face

as your heart knows,

this is the secret

to living a fulfilled life.

TENDING TO

Each tiny grain of sand
can become a pearl
when tended to
with love, care and nourishment.

It is a delicate dance
of patience, attention and intention
that fosters the conditions for opulence.
And it is possible
every single time
there is a wave of inspiration.

Ride it toward expansion

where you will find freedom

the great buffer.

Here,
an effortless
contraction and expansion
creates a dynamic play
of give and take

that places layer upon layer
of iridescence
until a magnificent creation
is complete.

THE VOID

First you're here
and then you're not.
Whispers on the wind of change
allude to what happens next.

There is an emptiness now
a void
a pause.

Patience
and breath
are all that remain
in the void.

SIMPLY BE

There is an emptiness
between what happened
and what happens next
where everything resides.

Be careful
not to let the waves
of loneliness pull you under
for too long.

Look to the surface
for the light

that will always guide you
home.

It is uncomfortable here.
And if you can trust
that this is the fertile ground
for creation,
perhaps you can soften
and allow a witnessing
of the darkness
to simply be.

There are no stories
to be told
in this place of emptiness

only silence

where the seeds of creation

are germinating

by the grace

of the Earth's hum.

FULL THROTTLE

It is so easy to fall in love with you.

Don't hold back I say.
I can fall in love with you
and it doesn't matter if you don't reciprocate
the fall.

I can fall in love with many you's.

The scent of the rain on the parched earth,

the way the warm ocean wind dances
with the hair upon my skin just after dark,

the wayward souls whispering to me
in the pre-dawn hours seeking company,

the graceful curves of the riverbed
among the red clay canyon walls,

a hawk's cry beckoning me to freedom.

I could easily fall in love with you

and so I do.

BE DAZZLED

My heart weeps
every time you touch me.

There is a sublime truth
that lies in the space
between your fingertips
and the surface of my skin.

A polarity tension
that electrifies
every cell
in my being.

Come to me now

so we can

be dazzled

by the divine interplay

of

conscious loving.

TRUTH OF MY SURRENDER

Any doubts I had

about not being able to fly

were incinerated

by the truth

of my surrender.

LOST TREASURES

You are welcome here.

You, are welcome here.

Come into my temple

where vastness allows

us to travel

to unknown depths

where we become

deep sea divers

excavating

long lost treasures

from the ancient sea beds

of our truest essence.

Together

we can dance

among the seaweed,

octopus and coral

as the whale songs

teach us

familiar melodies

of belonging.

Here in this temple,

we bow

at the feet

of the Divine Mother.

She rocks us to sleep

in her loving embrace

and we dream

of the stars

and days to come.

BLOSSOMING

Arise, arise
Beautiful One.

The time for your blossoming
is upon us.

Take my hand
and walk with me
as we traverse
galactic dimensions
and take hold of
that which will nourish you
into fruition.

We are here now
to gather
all that belongs
in your heart.

Allow it in
to bear the fruits
of your blossoming.

ANCESTORS

We ride upon the backs
of those that came before
only now
they have the courage
to uphold us.

All resistance is gone.

What remains is pure love
and celebration

for the paths

we choose to take

that lead us all

into

an expression of light.

CHILDREN OF THE STARS

You know me now.
You knew me once before.

This is not
the first time we've met.

We have traveled
lifetimes together
wizened by other places
and the other times
that taught us
how to embrace
the beauty of life.

149

An expansiveness of light
in our hearts
resounds now
only because
we have continued to say yes.

Despite the aches, the pains
our intentions remained
on freedom
of our heart's truest expression.

We pave the way
to this freedom
taking a stand
for exquisite belonging.

We are
children of the stars.

Our hearts beat as one
as we remember the times
we aligned and misaligned

that brought us
here now
together
again.

PURE PRESENCE

Awaken, Glorious One
the day is before you
where infinite possibilities
of magic reside.

Will you take moments
to pause and revel
in the divine miracle
of life?

You are here now.
What a blessing.

You are one

of a select few among so many

that gets to play

among the birds,

waterfalls, mountains,

and stars.

What are you waiting for?

What holds you back

from belly laughter,

dancing with wild abandon,

frolicking in play

among the dolphins in the waves?

You are here, now,

to experience

your sensual nature

at its fullest capacity

delighting

in the curiosity of each moment.

There is something precious

to be found here

in this place

of pure presence.

ASTOUND ME WITH
YOUR LOVE

You astound me
with your love.

From the moment
your eyes met mine
you commanded presence
in the gentlest of ways.

We played
with fire
burning brightly
between us.

An inferno,
a purifying flame
dissolving any pain
left in the heart.

You took my breath
away
again and again.

Returning it greater than before
a fuel source
powering the turbines
of a shattered heart
reassembled, strengthened
by the golden seams
binding
the fault lines
of life.

SILENCE OF THE HEART

Be here now

in all the pain, sadness

and joy.

In the fullness

of your presence

you will find

the waves

will always

eventually subside.

157

In the calm

remains

the silence

of the heart.

FRUITS OF YOU

The fruit of your skin

transports me

every time

the tip of my tongue

dances along

the crests

of you.

I savor every moment,

every taste of you

the finest fruit.

One tiny drop

is enough to
create explosions,
ecstatic waves
making turbulence,
shaking loose
any remains
of reservation or doubt.

I am a deeply sensual being
fully awakened now
by the sweetness of your flesh
and the decadence
of your soul.

REST HERE NOW

There's no sleep
with you beside me.

I hold your hand
smiling
for the blessings bestowed upon me
are many.

I trace the curves of your lips
the angle of your cheeks
with my eyes.

As I watch you sleep
inhaling and exhaling

the beauty of life
rests here now.

ALTITUDES

I watch you walk away.
I feel the most elated
and most devastated
I can remember feeling.

You took me to places
I've never known.
An altitude
where breathing
was constricted
by the pleasure of the inhale.

What happens now

that I've placed a flag
on this mountain peak?

With many more to climax
I wonder
will I see you there
again
among the mountain ranges
with the sun shining
upon your face
lighting up your eyes
with the fire
of a midsummer's dance?

Your smile
a sunburst of its own

from another galaxy
far from this one.

I will meet you here
again and again
to climb the highest altitudes
and watch the sun rise.

EARTHLY DELIGHTS

Earthly delights are many.

Each time the rain falls down
upon your skin
and tickles you with its cool kiss,

The silence of snowfall
glistening in aloneness,

The dance of the light
upon the water at high noon,

The band of milky ways

wrapping the night sky in glorious wonder.

Outside there is a child laughing,
inviting you to play.

Will you embrace
the bounty before you
and gratefully indulge
in the plenitude
of earthly delights?

LISTEN

Your heart
knows the way
to guide you
to places of wonder
that hold the keys
to every question
you want answered.

Enter this realm.
Ask.
And listen.

WILL YOU SURRENDER?

Will you surrender
control to me?

I will walk you
among the stars
where you can fly
freely
as you dance with the angels
to their rhythms of life.

I'll meet you
in the spaces in between
where pure potentiality

is abuzz, electric

And each next step
is born
out of the nothingness
and the everythingness

that full surrender
holds.

SLEEP LESS NOW

There is a whisper on the wind
enticing me to play.

I hear it calling me
in the late hours of the night.
Wake up, wake up
there will be plenty of time
for sleeping
when your time here is complete.

For now, delight and savor
moments of timeless beauty
that sing songs of sweetness
in your ears.

DON'T RUSH

Don't rush.

Allow breath and spaciousness

to guide you

in their wondrous ways.

They make everything

come to life

with their invitation

for presence.

FULLEST EXPRESSION

Last night
you gave me a great gift.

It was an invitation
to welcome home
parts of me
I didn't realize
were far removed
from the chambers of my heart.

From this newfound
place of wholeness

I leapt

courageously,

unabashedly

into the realms of the deep

where the most precious treasure

lie waiting for me

A key

to set

my voice free

to its fullest expression.

WE MADE STARS

A thousand thank yous
are easy to say
to you, my dear.

Grace moves through.
I love you
for seeing me and touching me
with the gentleness of your soul.

You've cracked me open
in the best of ways.
A return to wholeness
in your arms, under your weight.

We made stars last night
I found my way home
in your eyes.

The sweetness of our tears
divine harmony
dancing to the beat
throes of ecstasy.

You receive all of me
one petal at a time.
I receive all of you
this rose garden divine.

A thousand thank yous
does not quite convey

how grateful I am

for the way you love.

We made stars last night

I found my way home.

ABOUT THE AUTHOR

Kristen D'Amato can psychically see and intuitively know information about people's health concerns. For two decades, she's helped many relieve their symptoms without drugs and surgeries, inspiring empowerment in their healing journeys.

Kristen created the *Wheel of Whole Body Healing*, a wellness roadmap that places the power of healing back into the hands of the individual. Besides being the founder of Come to Life, a business centered on transformation through health and intimacy, Kristen is author of multiple books including, *We Choose Love: Redefining Our Relationship to Healing*. She holds a Master of Science in Mind-Body Medicine with a certificate in Contemplative End-of-Life Care and is a doctoral researcher in Mind-Body Medicine, a certified sex & relationship coach and a trained energy medicine practitioner.

Kristen is also a mother, musician, dancer, nature

179

lover, artist and passionate devotee of living an ecstatic life. She believes every person has valuable gifts that contribute to the well-being of the global community and aims to guide as many people as possible to live the fullest expression of their gifts for maximum joy and vitality.

To purchase books or for more information about programs, keynote speaking, and working directly with Kristen, visit kristendamato.com.

ABOUT COME TO LIFE

Our mission at Come to Life is to uplift, empower, and teach others to consciously co-create with their body's innate ability to heal through education, listening, acceptance, kindness, and love.

Our work is grounded in transformation through embodiment. We guide others toward a sense of absolute belonging to their bodies, to their communities, to each other, and to our planet.

To learn more about Come to Life's online programs and customized wellness experiences, visit wecometolife.com.

www.ingramcontent.com/pod-product-compliance
Lightning Source LLC
Chambersburg PA
CBHW020452130626
46549CB00001B/392